THE PLAYFUL PATH

Full-Title

Copyright

Dedication

Dedicated to all of those who bravely face the world despite fear and pain. You make the world a brighter place just by showing up.

Contents

1

Foreword

As a life coach who has navigated the complex and often misunderstood waters of Rejection Sensitive Dysphoria (RSD), I understand intimately the challenges it presents. In this journey, I've discovered that the power of playfulness, humor, and joy can be transformative. It's a path less traveled, yet immensely rewarding.

In "The Playful Path: Navigating Rejection Sensitive Dysphoria with Humor and Joy," I aim to offer not just a guide, but a companion for those who feel overwhelmed by the intense emotional responses characteristic of RSD. This book is a testament to the resilience of the human spirit, a narrative that unfolds the possibility of turning vulnerability into strength.

Throughout my career as a life coach, I have met countless individuals who, like me, experience the world with heightened sensitivity. This sensitivity, while often perceived as a hurdle, can be a profound source of empathy, creativity, and insight.

Embracing it with a playful heart and a joyful spirit is not just an act of courage; it's an act of rebellion against the norms that dictate how we should perceive our emotional landscape.

In these pages, you will find not only my personal reflections and experiences but also practical strategies to cultivate a life filled with laughter, lightness, and self-acceptance. We delve into the

art of transforming the fear of rejection into opportunities for personal growth and happiness.

This book is a call to those who feel deeply — to not just navigate but dance through the tides of Rejection Sensitive Dysphoria. It is an invitation to embrace your authentic self, to laugh a little louder, and to find joy in the everyday.

Welcome to "The Playful Path." Let's embark on this journey together, with hearts open to the laughter and light that await us.

Table of Contents

Chapter 1: Understanding Rejection Sensitive Dysphoria

What is Rejection Sensitive Dysphoria?

Rejection Sensitive Dysphoria (RSD) is a condition characterized by an extreme sensitivity to perceived rejection or criticism. People with RSD often experience intense emotional reactions, such as sadness, anger, or anxiety, in response to situations that may be perceived as rejection or disapproval. This emotional response can be triggered by a variety of social interactions, including dating, friendships, and other social settings.

Living with RSD can be challenging, as it can make it difficult to form and maintain relationships, both romantic and platonic. However, it is important to remember that having RSD does not mean you cannot have a joyous, fun, and fulfilling life. With the right strategies and techniques, it is possible to navigate social interactions and develop a funny and outgoing personality.

One key aspect of managing RSD is finding joy and playfulness in social interactions despite rejection sensitivity. This involves learning to separate perceived rejection from actual rejection and focusing on the positive aspects of social interactions. By shifting your mindset and embracing a playful attitude, you can create a safe and adventurous environment for yourself and others.

When it comes to dating, individuals with RSD may benefit from creating safe and adventurous dates. This can involve choosing activities that allow for open communication and vulnerability, while also providing an element of excitement and adventure. By setting clear boundaries and communicating your needs, you can navigate the dating world with confidence and self-assurance.

Nurturing friendships with RSD requires tips for being outgoing and developing a funny and humorous personality while managing rejection sensitivity. Building confidence and resilience in social settings is crucial, and enhancing communication skills can help individuals with RSD navigate dating and friendships more effectively. Self-care techniques, such as practicing mindfulness and engaging in activities that bring joy and fulfillment, are also important for managing RSD.

In conclusion, while living with RSD can present unique challenges, it is possible to have a joyous and fun-filled life. By understanding and managing rejection sensitivity, developing communication skills, and practicing self-care, individuals with RSD can cultivate fulfilling relationships, embrace adventure and excitement, and create a life that is full of joy and happiness.

Common Symptoms and Challenges

Living with rejection sensitive dysphoria (RSD) can present various symptoms and challenges that can make social interactions and relationships difficult. Understanding these common experiences can help individuals with RSD navigate their daily lives while still finding joy, playfulness, and adventure. In this subchapter, we will explore the symptoms and challenges faced by people with RSD and provide practical strategies for overcoming them.

One of the most prevalent symptoms of RSD is a heightened sensitivity to perceived rejection or criticism. Individuals with RSD often interpret neutral or even positive feedback as rejection, leading to feelings of intense emotional pain. This can result in social withdrawal, fear of rejection, and a reluctance to engage in new relationships or experiences. Additionally, individuals with RSD may struggle with low self-esteem, anxiety, and depression, further exacerbating their difficulties in social settings.

Despite these challenges, it is possible to cultivate a joyous, fun, and outgoing personality while managing RSD. By implementing self-care techniques and building resilience, individuals can learn to navigate rejection and develop a humorous and adventurous approach to life. Strategies such as mindfulness, practicing self-compassion, and seeking support can help manage the emotional rollercoaster that comes with RSD.

When it comes to dating and friendships, individuals with RSD may face unique obstacles. Fear of rejection may hinder their ability to initiate and maintain relationships. However, by creating safe and adventurous dates, individuals can gradually build their confidence and overcome their fears. Enhancing communication skills, such as active listening and assertiveness, can also improve relationships and reduce the impact of rejection sensitivity.

Nurturing friendships with RSD requires understanding and open communication. Friends who are aware of an individual's challenges can provide support and create a safe environment for social interactions. Additionally, developing a funny and humorous personality can be a powerful tool in navigating rejection, as laughter can help diffuse tension and create connection.

In conclusion, although RSD poses its own set of challenges, it is possible to lead a fulfilling and joyful life. By implementing self-care techniques, building resilience, improving communication skills, and seeking support, individuals with RSD can overcome their fear of rejection and embrace the adventures that life has to offer. With a playful and outgoing attitude, they can create meaningful relationships, enjoy exciting experiences, and find laughter in the face of rejection.

2

Chapter 2: Overcoming Rejection Sensitivity in Social Interactions

Embracing Joy and Playfulness

In the face of rejection sensitive dysphoria, it can be challenging to embrace joy and playfulness in social interactions. The fear of rejection and the constant worry about how others perceive us can dampen our spirits and make it difficult to let loose and have fun. However, it is possible to cultivate a joyous, fun, and playful mindset despite RSD. In this subchapter, we will explore various strategies and techniques that can help individuals with rejection sensitive dysphoria find joy and playfulness in their lives.

One of the first steps to embracing joy and playfulness is to understand that rejection is not a reflection of your worth as a person. It is crucial to separate your self-esteem from the opinions and judgments of others. Remember that everyone experiences rejection at some point, and it does not define who you are. By shifting your mindset and focusing on your own self-worth, you can begin to let go of the fear of rejection and open yourself up to joy and playfulness.

Creating safe and adventurous dates is another way to infuse joy and playfulness into your life despite rejection sensitivity. Instead of focusing on the potential for rejection, try to approach dating as an opportunity for new experiences and personal growth. Plan activities that you genuinely enjoy and that allow you to showcase your unique personality. By focusing on the enjoyment of the moment rather than the outcome, you can create a positive and fun-filled atmosphere.

Nurturing friendships can also contribute to a joyous and playful life. Surrounding yourself with supportive and understanding friends can help alleviate the fear of rejection. Be open and honest about your RSD with your friends, and seek their understanding and support. Engage in activities that make you feel happy and fulfilled, and allow yourself to be spontaneous and playful in their company.

Developing a funny and humorous personality while managing rejection sensitivity is possible with practice and self-compassion. Use humor as a coping mechanism and a way to connect with others. Embrace your unique sense of humor and don't be afraid to laugh at yourself. By finding the lightness in difficult situations, you can create a more joyful and playful outlook on life.

In conclusion, despite rejection sensitive dysphoria, it is possible to have a joyous, fun, and playful life. By shifting your mindset, creating safe and adventurous experiences, nurturing friendships, developing a humorous personality, and embracing self-care techniques, you can enhance your overall well-being and find joy in social interactions. Remember that rejection does not define you, and that you are deserving of love, friendship, and happiness. So, go forth, embrace joy, and playfulness, and live a fun-filled life despite rejection sensitivity.

Strategies for Dealing with Rejection

Rejection can be a challenging experience for anyone, but for individuals with rejection sensitive dysphoria (RSD), it can be particularly overwhelming and distressing. However, it is possible to develop strategies that can help you navigate these situations and find joy and playfulness in social interactions, dating, friendships, and daily life. In this subchapter, we will explore various techniques and approaches to help you embrace a joyous, fun-filled life despite rejection sensitive dysphoria.

1. Understanding RSD: Begin by gaining a deeper understanding of rejection sensitive dysphoria. Educate yourself about its symptoms, triggers, and impact on your emotions and behavior. This knowledge will enable you to better manage and cope with rejection.

2. Building Resilience: Developing resilience is crucial for navigating rejection. Focus on building your self-esteem and confidence through positive self-talk, self-care, and affirmations. Remember that rejection does not define your worth as a person.

3. Cultivating a Supportive Network: Surround yourself with friends and loved ones who understand and support you. Having a strong support system can provide comfort and encouragement during times of rejection.

4. Embracing Humor: Develop a funny and humorous personality as a way to cope with rejection. Laughing at yourself and finding humor in situations can help diffuse tension and boost your confidence.

5. Practicing Self-Care: Engage in activities that bring you joy and relaxation. Practice self-care techniques such as meditation, exercise, and hobbies that help you manage stress and maintain a positive mindset.

6. Enhancing Communication Skills: Work on improving your communication skills to effectively express your thoughts, feelings, and boundaries. Clear and assertive communication can help prevent misunderstandings and reduce the likelihood of rejection.

7. Taking Safe and Adventurous Steps: Push yourself out of your comfort zone by taking small, safe steps towards new experiences and adventures. Gradually expose yourself to situations that may trigger rejection, and celebrate your progress along the way.

8. Learning from Rejection: Instead of dwelling on rejection, focus on the lessons you can learn from these experiences. Use rejection as an opportunity for growth and self-improvement.

Remember, rejection sensitive dysphoria does not have to define your life. By implementing these strategies, you can develop a funny, outgoing personality, nurture meaningful friendships, and enjoy fulfilling relationships. Embrace the joy and playfulness that life has to offer, despite the challenges of rejection sensitivity.

3

Chapter 3: Dating and Making Friends with Rejection Sensitive Dysphoria

Creating Safe and Adventurous Dates

When you have rejection sensitive dysphoria, the thought of going on a date can be anxiety-inducing. The fear of rejection can make it challenging to put yourself out there and enjoy social interactions. However, with a little planning and the right mindset, you can have a joyous, fun, and adventurous time while navigating rejection sensitive dysphoria in dating.

First and foremost, it's essential to prioritize your safety. Before meeting someone new, ensure you have done a thorough background check. Utilize online platforms to gather information and get a sense of the person's character. Trust your intuition and only proceed if you feel comfortable and secure. Remember, your safety should always be the top priority.

Once you have found someone you'd like to go on a date with, choose activities that align with your interests and comfort level. Consider engaging in outdoor activities like hiking, biking, or exploring a new park. These activities provide an opportunity to bond, have fun, and create lasting memories while managing rejection sensitivity.

Communication is key when planning dates. Let your potential partner know about your rejection sensitive dysphoria and any specific triggers you may have. This will allow them to understand your needs and help create a safe and supportive environment for both of you.

When on the date, focus on enjoying the moment rather than worrying about potential rejection. Practice mindfulness and stay present. Embrace the adventure and excitement that comes with meeting new people and trying new things. Remember, rejection is a part of life, but it doesn't define you. Embrace rejection as a learning experience and an opportunity for personal growth.

Another important aspect of creating safe and adventurous dates is setting boundaries. Be clear about your comfort levels and communicate them openly. Don't be afraid to say no or voice your concerns if something doesn't feel right. Your well-being should always be respected and prioritized.

Lastly, surround yourself with supportive friends who understand your rejection sensitive dysphoria. Nurturing friendships will provide a strong support system and encourage you to be outgoing and funny. These friends can offer guidance, advice, and a listening ear when you need it most.

In conclusion, while rejection sensitive dysphoria may present challenges in dating, it is possible to have a joyous, fun, and adventurous time. Prioritize safety, communicate openly, set boundaries, and surround yourself with supportive friends. Embrace rejection as an opportunity for personal growth, and remember to enjoy the journey, regardless of the outcome. You deserve love, laughter, and a fulfilling dating life, regardless of rejection sensitivity.

Nurturing Friendships and Being Outgoing

Developing and maintaining friendships can be challenging for individuals with rejection sensitive dysphoria (RSD). The fear of rejection and criticism can make it difficult to open up and connect with others. However, with the right strategies and mindset, it is possible to have joyous, fun, and fulfilling social interactions. In this chapter, we will explore tips and techniques for nurturing friendships and being outgoing, even with RSD.

One of the first steps in nurturing friendships is to understand and accept your RSD. By acknowledging that rejection sensitivity is a part of your life, you can start to develop coping mechanisms and self-care techniques that will help you navigate social interactions. Practice self-compassion and remind yourself that everyone faces rejection at some point.

Building confidence and resilience is crucial when it comes to being outgoing. Start by setting small, achievable goals for yourself in social situations. Challenge your negative thoughts and replace them with positive affirmations. Surround yourself with supportive and understanding friends who can provide a safe and non-judgmental space for you to be yourself.

Communication skills play a vital role in developing and maintaining friendships. Practice active listening, show genuine interest in others, and be mindful of your body language. Be open and honest about your RSD with your friends, as this can foster understanding and empathy.

Creating safe and adventurous dates can also be a challenge for individuals with RSD. Start by planning activities that align with your interests and comfort level. Focus on shared experiences that promote laughter and joy. Remember, it's okay to take things slow and communicate your boundaries to your date.

Developing a funny and humorous personality can help alleviate the anxiety and fear of rejection. Find opportunities to laugh and be playful, both with friends and potential romantic partners. Embrace your unique sense of humor and use it as a tool to connect with others.

Lastly, self-care is essential for individuals with RSD. Take time for yourself to recharge and practice self-soothing techniques when faced with rejection. Surround yourself with positive influences and engage in activities that bring you joy and fulfillment.

In conclusion, nurturing friendships and being outgoing is possible, even with rejection sensitive dysphoria. By understanding and accepting your RSD, building confidence, enhancing communication skills, and practicing self-care, you can create joyous, fun-filled social interactions and develop meaningful connections with others. Remember, you are worthy of love, friendship, and laughter, regardless of rejection sensitivity.

4
=

Chapter 4: Developing a Funny and Outgoing Personality

Managing Rejection Sensitivity while Being Funny

Rejection sensitive dysphoria can make social interactions challenging and daunting, but it doesn't mean you can't have a joyous, fun, and outgoing personality. In fact, developing a funny and humorous side can help you navigate through rejection sensitivity and build strong relationships. In this subchapter, we will explore techniques and strategies to help you manage rejection sensitivity while still being funny and outgoing.

One of the first steps in managing rejection sensitivity is to understand your triggers and develop coping mechanisms. By identifying situations or behaviors that trigger your RSD, you can better prepare yourself for potential rejection. This self-awareness allows you to develop strategies to handle rejection in a healthy and constructive way. For example, instead of immediately shutting down or becoming defensive when faced with rejection, you can choose to respond with humor and light-heartedness, diffusing tension and creating a more positive atmosphere.

Humor can be a powerful tool in overcoming rejection sensitivity. By incorporating humor into your interactions, you can create a safe and playful environment that encourages open communication. Jokes and funny anecdotes can help break the ice and establish a connection with others, making it easier to navigate through potential rejection. However, it's important to remember that humor should always be used respectfully and in a way that doesn't belittle or offend others.

Another aspect to consider is self-care. Rejection sensitivity can take a toll on your emotional well-being, so it's crucial to take care of yourself. Engaging in activities that bring you joy and relaxation can help boost your confidence and resilience in social settings. Whether it's practicing mindfulness, engaging in hobbies, or seeking support from loved ones, self-care plays a vital role in managing rejection sensitivity while maintaining a funny and outgoing personality.

Building strong friendships and romantic relationships can also be challenging for individuals with rejection sensitivity. However, by enhancing your communication skills, you can foster deeper connections and navigate through potential rejection with grace. Active listening, empathy, and effective expression of emotions are key components in building successful relationships. Learning and practicing these skills can help you overcome the fear of rejection and foster meaningful connections.

In conclusion, managing rejection sensitivity while being funny and outgoing is possible. By understanding your triggers, developing coping mechanisms, incorporating humor, practicing self-care, and enhancing your communication skills, you can navigate social interactions with confidence and joy. Remember, rejection is a part of life, but it doesn't define your worth. With the right mindset and strategies, you can create a joyous and fun-filled life despite rejection sensitive dysphoria.

Using Humor to Connect with Others

Humor is a powerful tool that can help break down barriers and create connections with others. For individuals with rejection sensitive dysphoria (RSD), incorporating humor into social interactions can be a valuable way to navigate relationships, date, and make friends. In this subchapter, we will explore how to have a joyous, fun, and playful time, despite having rejection sensitive dysphoria, while finding joy and playfulness in social interactions.

Humor has the ability to lighten the atmosphere, ease tension, and create a sense of camaraderie. When used appropriately, it can help individuals with RSD feel more comfortable and confident in social settings. Here are some tips for incorporating humor into your interactions:

1. Embrace self-deprecating humor: Laughing at yourself can help put others at ease and show that you don't take yourself too seriously. It also demonstrates vulnerability, which can foster deeper connections.

2. Use lighthearted banter: Engaging in playful teasing can create a sense of camaraderie and rapport. However, it's important to ensure that your humor is received positively and doesn't inadvertently hurt or offend others.

3. Share funny anecdotes: Everyone loves a good story, especially one that brings a smile or a laugh. Sharing humorous experiences can help build connections and create shared experiences.

4. Use witty comebacks: Developing quick-witted responses can help you navigate difficult or awkward situations with humor. This can help diffuse tension and show your ability to think on your feet.

5. Appreciate the absurd: Finding humor in everyday situations can help you see the lighter side of life. Embrace the unexpected and learn to laugh at the absurdities that come your way.

Remember, humor should be used as a tool to connect and uplift others, rather than as a defense mechanism or a means to mask your true emotions. It's important to be sensitive to others' boundaries and ensure that your humor is inclusive, respectful, and appropriate for the situation.

By incorporating humor into your interactions, you can create a more enjoyable and fulfilling social life. Whether it's on a date, with friends, or in any social setting, a funny and outgoing personality can help you navigate rejection sensitive dysphoria while building confidence, resilience, and meaningful connections. So, embrace your sense of humor, have fun, and laugh in the face of rejection!

5

Chapter 5: Self-Care Techniques for Individuals with Rejection Sensitive Dysphoria

Practicing Mindfulness and Relaxation

In the journey of developing a funny and outgoing personality with rejection sensitive dysphoria (RSD), it is essential to prioritize self-care and emotional well-being. One powerful tool that can greatly support individuals with RSD is the practice of mindfulness and relaxation techniques. By incorporating these practices into your daily life, you can cultivate a sense of calm, resilience, and joy, even in the face of rejection.

Mindfulness is the practice of bringing your attention to the present moment without judgment. It allows you to observe your thoughts and emotions without getting caught up in them. By becoming more aware of your thoughts and feelings, you can gain a better understanding of how RSD affects you and develop strategies to navigate challenging situations.

One effective technique for practicing mindfulness is deep breathing. Take a moment to sit comfortably, close your eyes, and take a deep breath in through your nose. Allow the breath to fill your lungs, and then slowly exhale through your mouth. As you focus on your breath, notice how your body feels, any tension or discomfort, and simply let it go with each exhalation. This simple practice can help you ground yourself and find a sense of calm amidst the chaos of rejection sensitivity.

In addition to mindfulness, incorporating relaxation techniques into your routine can help reduce stress and anxiety. Engaging in activities such as meditation, yoga, or listening to soothing music can provide a much-needed break from the pressures of social interactions. These practices allow you to connect with yourself, release tension, and recharge your energy.

Remember, it's essential to create a safe and supportive environment for yourself. Set realistic expectations and boundaries when it comes to socializing, dating, and forming friendships. Surround yourself with people who understand and accept you for who you are, embracing your unique qualities, including RSD.

By practicing mindfulness and relaxation, you can develop the resilience and confidence needed to navigate social situations with joy and playfulness. Remember, rejection does not define you. Embrace your humor, explore new adventures, and foster meaningful connections. With self-care and a positive mindset, you can lead a joyous and fun-filled life, regardless of rejection sensitive dysphoria.

Building a Supportive Self-Care Routine

Living with rejection sensitive dysphoria (RSD) can be challenging, but it doesn't mean you can't have a joyous, fun, and adventurous life. In fact, developing a supportive self-care routine can help you navigate social interactions, build confidence, and find joy and playfulness despite rejection sensitivity.

One of the first steps in building a supportive self-care routine is to prioritize your mental and emotional well-being. This means taking time for yourself and engaging in activities that bring you joy and relaxation. Whether it's reading a book, taking a bath, or practicing mindfulness, finding activities that help you de-stress and recharge is essential.

Another important aspect of self-care for individuals with RSD is nurturing friendships and building a strong support network. Surrounding yourself with understanding and compassionate friends can make a world of difference. Seek out people who appreciate your unique qualities, support your growth, and understand your struggles.

When it comes to dating, it's important to create safe and adventurous experiences that align with your comfort level. Start by setting boundaries and communicating your needs and limitations with potential partners. Remember, it's okay to take things at your own pace and prioritize your emotional well-being.

Developing a funny and outgoing personality while managing rejection sensitivity may seem daunting, but it's possible. Embrace your sense of humor and use it as a tool to navigate social situations. Find ways to make light of rejection and laugh at yourself. This not only helps you cope with rejection but also allows others to see your resilient and humorous side.

Enhancing communication skills is another crucial aspect of self-care for individuals with RSD. Practice active listening, empathy, and assertiveness when interacting with others. Effective communication can help you express your needs, set boundaries, and build stronger connections.

Lastly, remember that rejection sensitive dysphoria doesn't define you. It's important to embrace your unique qualities and celebrate your strengths. Focus on the things you love about yourself and cultivate self-compassion. This will help you build confidence and resilience in social settings.

In conclusion, developing a supportive self-care routine is essential for individuals with rejection sensitive dysphoria. By prioritizing your mental and emotional well-being, nurturing friendships, creating safe and adventurous experiences, developing a funny and outgoing personality, enhancing communication skills, and embracing your unique qualities, you can live a joyous and fun-filled life despite rejection sensitivity. Laugh in the face of rejection and thrive!

6

Chapter 6: Building Confidence and Resilience in Social Settings

Overcoming Fear of Rejection

Rejection can be a daunting prospect for anyone, but for individuals with rejection sensitive dysphoria (RSD), it can feel even more overwhelming. The fear of rejection can be paralyzing, affecting your ability to form meaningful relationships and enjoy social interactions. However, it is possible to overcome this fear and develop a joyful, fun, and adventurous personality, even with RSD.

One of the first steps in overcoming the fear of rejection is understanding that rejection is not a reflection of your worth as a person. It is crucial to separate the rejection from your identity and remind yourself that it is simply a part of life. Everyone faces rejection at some point, and it does not define who you are.

Another important aspect is embracing a playful and lighthearted attitude towards social interactions. Instead of approaching situations with fear and anxiety, try to view them as opportunities for growth and learning. Emphasize the fun and enjoyment that can come from connecting with others, rather than solely focusing on the fear of rejection.

Creating safe and adventurous dates can also help individuals with RSD navigate the dating scene. By choosing activities that align with your interests and comfort levels, you can foster an environment where you feel at ease. This will allow you to be more open and authentic, increasing the chances of forming genuine connections.

In nurturing friendships, it is essential to be outgoing. Take small steps to initiate conversations and socialize with others. Developing a funny and humorous personality can be an effective way to break the ice, as laughter can help alleviate tension and create a positive atmosphere.

Self-care techniques play a vital role in managing rejection sensitivity. Prioritize activities that bring you joy and help you relax, such as practicing mindfulness, engaging in hobbies, or seeking therapy. Building confidence and resilience in social settings may also involve challenging yourself to step outside your comfort zone gradually.

Effective communication skills are essential for individuals with rejection sensitive dysphoria in both dating and friendships. Learning how to express your needs, set boundaries, and actively listen to others can foster healthy and meaningful connections.

Ultimately, overcoming the fear of rejection with rejection sensitive dysphoria requires a combination of self-acceptance, humor, and resilience. By embracing a playful and adventurous mindset, nurturing friendships, and practicing self-care, it is possible to enjoy a joyous and fulfilling life, despite the challenges of rejection sensitivity. Remember, rejection does not define you – it is simply a stepping stone on the path to personal growth and connection.

Building Confidence through Positive Self-Talk

Rejection sensitive dysphoria (RSD) can make it challenging to navigate social situations, form connections, and express oneself freely. However, it doesn't have to hold you back from living a joyous, fun-filled life filled with meaningful friendships and romantic relationships.

In this subchapter, we will explore the power of positive self-talk in building confidence and overcoming the hurdles that come with RSD.

Positive self-talk is a technique that involves intentionally replacing negative, self-defeating thoughts with positive and affirming ones. By actively changing the way you think about yourself and your abilities, you can cultivate a mindset that empowers you to face rejection with resilience and maintain an outgoing and funny personality.

Firstly, it's important to recognize that rejection is a normal part of life. Everyone, regardless of whether they have RSD or not, experiences rejection at some point. Remind yourself that a rejection does not define your worth as a person. Instead of dwelling on negative thoughts such as "I'm unlikable" or "I'll never fit in," replace them with statements like "I am deserving of love and friendship" or "I have unique qualities that others appreciate."

Another effective technique is to reframe your thoughts by focusing on the positive aspects of a situation. For instance, if you experience rejection while dating or making new friends, instead of internalizing it as a personal failure, remind yourself that it's an opportunity to learn and grow. Tell yourself, "I am brave for putting myself out there, and I will continue to meet new people who appreciate me for who I am."

Additionally, practicing self-compassion is crucial when dealing with RSD. Treat yourself with kindness and understanding, just as you would a close friend. Acknowledge that setbacks and rejections happen to everyone, and use them as opportunities for personal development. Replace self-critical thoughts with compassionate statements like "I am doing my best, and that's enough" or "I am resilient and capable of bouncing back from any rejection."

Remember, building confidence is a process that takes time and effort. Surround yourself with a support system of friends, family, or even a therapist who can provide encouragement and help you challenge negative self-talk. By consciously monitoring and adjusting your internal dialogue, you can slowly rewire your brain to embrace a more positive and resilient mindset.

In conclusion, developing a funny, outgoing personality while managing rejection sensitive dysphoria is possible. Through the power of positive self-talk, you can build confidence, form meaningful connections, and navigate social situations with grace. Embrace your unique qualities, learn from setbacks, and practice self-compassion. Laugh in the face of rejection and watch as your joyous, playful, and adventurous self shines through.

7

Chapter 7: Navigating Adventure and Excitement in Relationships

Exploring New Experiences and Activities

In this subchapter, we will delve into the realm of new experiences and activities, and how individuals with rejection sensitive dysphoria (RSD) can embrace joy, playfulness, and adventure in their lives. Despite the challenges posed by RSD, it is possible to have a fulfilling and enjoyable social life, establish meaningful friendships, and even date with confidence and humor. By adopting certain strategies and implementing self-care techniques, individuals with RSD can navigate rejection and cultivate resilience while exploring new avenues of excitement.

One key aspect to finding joy and playfulness in social interactions despite rejection sensitivity is to approach them with a light-hearted and humorous attitude. Developing a funny and outgoing personality can help ease the fear of rejection and create a more relaxed atmosphere. Incorporating humor into conversations, practicing witty comebacks, and embracing spontaneity can all contribute to a more enjoyable social experience.

When it comes to dating, individuals with RSD may find it challenging to create safe and adventurous experiences. However, by communicating their needs and boundaries clearly, they can ensure that their dating experiences are both enjoyable and comfortable. Planning activities that are low-pressure, such as going for a walk or trying a new hobby together, can help alleviate anxiety and foster a sense of connection.

Nurturing friendships with rejection sensitive dysphoria requires being outgoing and proactive. Tips for building friendships include reaching out to others, joining social groups or clubs, and engaging in activities that align with personal interests. By focusing on shared interests and maintaining open lines of communication, individuals with RSD can establish strong and supportive friendships.

In order to navigate rejection sensitive dysphoria in relationships, it is important to explore adventure and excitement while also prioritizing self-care. Engaging in activities that bring joy and fulfillment, such as pursuing hobbies or practicing mindfulness, can help individuals maintain a sense of balance and resilience in the face of rejection.

Enhancing communication skills is another crucial aspect of developing fulfilling relationships and friendships. By practicing active listening, expressing oneself clearly and honestly, and seeking to understand others' perspectives, individuals with RSD can build stronger connections and reduce the fear of rejection.

Overall, despite the challenges presented by rejection sensitive dysphoria, it is possible to live a joyous and fun-filled life. By adopting strategies for self-care, building confidence and resilience, and embracing new experiences and activities, individuals with RSD can navigate rejection with grace and develop meaningful connections with others. Remember, a playful and adventurous spirit can overcome the fear of rejection and open doors to a world of possibilities.

Overcoming Fear of Rejection in Romantic Relationships

In the journey of finding joy and fulfillment in romantic relationships, individuals with rejection sensitive dysphoria (RSD) often face unique challenges. The fear of rejection can be overwhelming, leading to feelings of anxiety, self-doubt, and a reluctance to put oneself out there. However, by developing a funny and outgoing personality, individuals with RSD can overcome their fear of rejection and create meaningful connections.

One of the first steps in overcoming the fear of rejection is to understand that rejection is not a reflection of one's worth or value. Rejection is a natural part of life, and everyone experiences it at some point. By reframing rejection as an opportunity for growth and learning, individuals with RSD can approach romantic relationships with a more positive mindset.

Another helpful strategy is to embrace humor and playfulness in social interactions. Laughter can be a powerful tool in diffusing tension and creating a sense of connection. By developing a funny and humorous personality, individuals with RSD can create a safe and enjoyable environment for themselves and their potential partners.

Creating safe and adventurous dates is another way to overcome the fear of rejection. By planning activities that are fun and exciting, individuals with RSD can shift their focus away from the fear of rejection and towards having a good time. This can help build confidence and resilience in social settings.

Nurturing friendships is also crucial for individuals with RSD. Having a support system of friends who understand and accept them can boost self-esteem and provide a sense of belonging. By being outgoing and open to new friendships, individuals with RSD can build a network of supportive relationships that can help them navigate the challenges of romantic relationships.

Effective communication skills are essential in overcoming the fear of rejection. By expressing oneself confidently and assertively, individuals with RSD can ensure that their needs and desires are heard and understood. Building these skills takes practice, but with time and effort, individuals with RSD can enhance their communication abilities and foster healthier and more fulfilling relationships.

Above all, it is vital for individuals with RSD to practice self-care. Taking time for oneself, engaging in activities that bring joy and fulfillment, and seeking professional help when needed are all important steps in managing RSD and overcoming the fear of rejection.

In conclusion, by developing a funny and outgoing personality, individuals with rejection sensitive dysphoria can overcome their fear of rejection in romantic relationships. Through embracing humor and playfulness, creating safe and adventurous dates, nurturing friendships, developing effective communication skills, and practicing self-care, individuals with RSD can find joy and fulfillment in their social interactions and create meaningful connections.

8

Chapter 8: Enhancing Communication Skills in Dating and Friendships

Active Listening and Empathy

In the realm of social interactions, one of the most powerful tools you can possess is the ability to actively listen and empathize with others. This skill becomes even more crucial for individuals with rejection sensitive dysphoria (RSD), as it allows you to navigate relationships, friendships, and dating with confidence and authenticity.

Active listening involves not only hearing the words someone is saying but also understanding their emotions, intentions, and underlying needs. It requires being fully present in the moment, giving your undivided attention, and genuinely seeking to understand the other person. By actively listening, you create a safe space for open and honest communication, which is essential for building strong connections.

Empathy goes hand in hand with active listening. It is the ability to put yourself in someone else's shoes, to understand and share their feelings and experiences. Empathy allows you to connect on a deeper level with others, fostering trust and genuine understanding. When you empathize, you validate the other person's emotions, letting them know that their feelings are heard and respected.

For individuals with RSD, active listening and empathy can be particularly challenging. The fear of rejection may make it difficult to fully engage in conversations, as you may be preoccupied with worrying about how others perceive you. However, by practicing these skills, you can break free from the constraints of rejection sensitivity and create meaningful and fulfilling relationships.

To cultivate active listening and empathy, start by focusing on the person in front of you. Put away distractions and give them your undivided attention. Maintain eye contact and use nonverbal cues, such as nodding and leaning in, to show that you are fully present and engaged. Practice reflective listening by summarizing and paraphrasing what the other person has said to ensure understanding.

When it comes to empathy, take the time to truly listen to the emotions behind someone's words. Try to imagine how they might be feeling and validate their experiences. Use phrases like, "It sounds like you're feeling..." or "I can understand why that would be difficult for you." By demonstrating empathy, you create a safe and supportive environment where others feel valued and understood.

Remember, developing active listening and empathy is a lifelong journey. It takes practice and patience, but the rewards are immeasurable. By honing these skills, you can forge deep and meaningful connections, navigate rejection sensitivity with grace, and create a joyous and fulfilling life filled with laughter and adventure.

Assertiveness and Setting Boundaries

Assertiveness and setting boundaries are essential skills for individuals with rejection sensitive dysphoria (RSD) to navigate social interactions, build relationships, and create a joyous and playful life. By developing these skills, individuals can overcome the fear of rejection and cultivate healthy connections with others.

One of the key aspects of assertiveness is expressing your needs and desires clearly and respectfully. It is important to communicate your boundaries to others, ensuring that your limits and comfort levels are respected. By asserting yourself, you can avoid being taken advantage of or compromising your emotional well-being. Remember, it is perfectly okay to prioritize your own happiness and mental health.

Setting boundaries can be challenging, especially for individuals with RSD who may fear rejection or conflict. However, establishing and maintaining healthy boundaries is crucial for building fulfilling relationships. Start by identifying your personal boundaries and what makes you feel comfortable or uncomfortable. Communicate these boundaries to others in a calm and assertive manner, using "I" statements to express your feelings and needs.

It is also important to listen to and respect the boundaries of others. By creating a mutual understanding and respect for each person's boundaries, you can foster healthier and more rewarding relationships. Remember that boundaries can evolve over time, so it is important to regularly check in with yourself and communicate any changes or adjustments to your boundaries.

In addition to assertiveness and setting boundaries, self-care is vital for individuals with RSD. Taking time for yourself, engaging in activities that bring you joy and relaxation, and practicing self-compassion can help manage rejection sensitivity and enhance your overall well-being. Remember to prioritize self-care and make it a regular part of your routine.

By developing assertiveness, setting boundaries, and practicing self-care, individuals with RSD can create a positive and fulfilling social life. Remember that rejection is a part of life and is not a reflection of your worth. Embrace your unique personality, find joy in social interactions, and cultivate meaningful connections with others. With these tools and strategies, you can overcome rejection sensitivity and live a joyous and fun-filled life.

9

Chapter 9: Strategies for Enjoying a Joyous and Fun-filled Life

Finding and Pursuing Hobbies and Passions

In the face of rejection sensitive dysphoria, it can be challenging to find joy and playfulness in social interactions. However, it is possible to cultivate a joyous, fun, and adventurous life, even with this condition. One way to achieve this is by discovering and pursuing hobbies and passions that bring you happiness and fulfillment.

Engaging in activities that you are passionate about can help divert your focus from the fear of rejection and allow you to explore your true interests. Whether it's painting, playing a musical instrument, writing, or dancing, finding a hobby that resonates with you can provide a sense of purpose and excitement.

When it comes to dating and friendships, it's essential to create safe and adventurous experiences that cater to your unique needs. Consider activities that allow you to feel comfortable and in control, such as going for a walk in a park, visiting a museum, or trying a new restaurant. By carefully selecting activities that align with your interests and comfort level, you can enhance your enjoyment and decrease the likelihood of triggering rejection sensitive dysphoria.

Nurturing friendships is crucial for individuals with rejection sensitive dysphoria. Tips for being outgoing include actively listening, showing genuine interest in others, and maintaining open and honest communication. By focusing on building strong connections with people who understand and support you, you can create a reliable and uplifting social network.

Developing a funny and humorous personality while managing rejection sensitivity is possible. Embrace your unique sense of humor and use it as a tool to lighten up social situations. Be willing to laugh at yourself and find the humor in everyday experiences. Not only can this help you connect with others, but it can also boost your confidence and resilience in social settings.

Self-care techniques are vital for individuals with rejection sensitive dysphoria in dating. Practice self-compassion, engage in relaxation exercises, and prioritize activities that bring you joy and relaxation. Taking care of yourself physically, emotionally, and mentally will contribute to your overall well-being and make dating experiences more enjoyable.

Enhancing communication skills is essential for navigating rejection sensitive dysphoria in dating and friendships. Be honest with yourself and others about your needs and boundaries. By effectively expressing yourself, you can foster understanding and build stronger connections.

Ultimately, strategies for enjoying a joyous and fun-filled life despite rejection sensitive dysphoria involve embracing your unique qualities, pursuing your passions, and surrounding yourself with supportive and understanding individuals. By focusing on self-care, building resilience, and cultivating meaningful relationships, you can create a fulfilling and adventurous life. Remember, rejection sensitive dysphoria does not define you – it is merely a part of your journey towards self-discovery and personal growth.

Cultivating Gratitude and Positive Thinking

In the face of rejection, it can be challenging to maintain a positive outlook and nurture a grateful mindset. However, by cultivating gratitude and positive thinking, individuals with rejection sensitive dysphoria (RSD) can find joy, playfulness, and adventure in their social interactions, relationships, and everyday life. In this subchapter, we will explore various strategies and techniques that can help you develop a funny and outgoing personality while managing rejection sensitivity.

One powerful tool for cultivating gratitude is keeping a gratitude journal. Each day, take a few moments to write down three things you are grateful for. It could be as simple as a beautiful sunset or a kind word from a friend. This practice trains your mind to focus on the positive aspects of your life, even when faced with rejection or disappointment.

Positive affirmations are another effective way to shift your mindset towards positivity. Create a list of affirmations that resonate with you and repeat them daily. For example, "I am worthy of love and friendship," or "I embrace rejection as an opportunity for growth." By affirming these positive statements, you can rewire your brain to believe in your own worth and abilities.

Engaging in activities that bring you joy and playfulness is vital for individuals with RSD. Find hobbies or interests that make you feel alive and incorporate them into your daily routine. Whether it's dancing, painting, or playing a musical instrument, these activities can boost your mood and help you develop a more outgoing and adventurous personality.

Building strong friendships and romantic relationships can be challenging for individuals with RSD. However, by focusing on effective communication and setting boundaries, you can foster meaningful connections. Practice active listening, empathy, and expressing your needs and desires openly. Remember that rejection is not a reflection of your worth; it is an opportunity to find the right people who appreciate and value you for who you are.

Finally, self-care is crucial for individuals with RSD. Take time to prioritize your physical, emotional, and mental well-being. Engage in activities that promote relaxation and reduce stress, such as meditation, yoga, or spending time in nature. Surround yourself with a support network of understanding and compassionate individuals who can provide encouragement and guidance.

By cultivating gratitude and positive thinking, individuals with RSD can overcome rejection sensitivity and develop a funny, outgoing personality. Embrace the joy, playfulness, and adventure that life has to offer, and remember that rejection is just a stepping stone towards personal growth and finding genuine connections. Laugh in the face of rejection and live a joyous, fulfilling life despite rejection sensitive dysphoria.

Chapter 10: Conclusion and Moving Forward with Confidence

Congratulations! You have reached the final chapter of "Laughing in the Face of Rejection: Developing a Funny and Outgoing Personality with RSD." Throughout this book, we have explored various strategies and techniques to help you navigate rejection sensitive dysphoria (RSD) and live a joyous, fun-filled life. In this concluding chapter, we will summarize key takeaways and provide guidance on how to continue your journey with confidence.

One of the main themes we have emphasized throughout this book is the importance of finding joy and playfulness in social interactions despite rejection sensitivity. Remember that rejection is a natural part of life, and it does not define your worth as a person. By embracing a positive mindset and focusing on the moments of laughter and connection, you can create a safe and adventurous environment for yourself and others.

When it comes to dating and forming friendships, rejection sensitive individuals often face unique challenges. However, don't let fear hold you back. Armed with the tools and techniques shared in this book, you can nurture relationships and be outgoing. Take small steps, be patient with yourself, and practice self-care techniques to manage any setbacks that may arise.

Building confidence and resilience in social settings is crucial for individuals with rejection sensitivity. Remember that confidence is not about being perfect, but about embracing your authentic self and accepting both your strengths and vulnerabilities. Practice effective communication skills, such as active listening and assertiveness, to enhance your interactions and build stronger connections.

As you continue your journey, don't forget to explore adventure and excitement in your relationships. It is possible to navigate rejection sensitive dysphoria while still having fun and enjoying new experiences. Keep an open mind, be willing to step out of your comfort zone, and embrace the unexpected. Remember, the path to personal growth often lies outside of our comfort zones.

In conclusion, "Laughing in the Face of Rejection" has provided you with a comprehensive guide to developing a funny and outgoing personality despite rejection sensitive dysphoria. By implementing the strategies and techniques discussed in this book, you can create a joyous and fun-filled life for yourself. Remember, you are not alone on this journey. Reach out to support networks, seek therapy if needed, and surround yourself with positive influences. With determination, resilience, and a sense of humor, you can overcome the challenges of rejection sensitivity and live your best life. So, go forth with confidence and embrace the endless possibilities that await you!

In Closing

As we reach the end of this journey together, I hope "The Playful Path: Navigating Rejection Sensitive Dysphoria with Humor and Joy" has offered you not just insights but also a sense of companionship in your own journey. Remember, embracing playfulness and joy in the face of RSD is a continuous process, one that unfolds uniquely for each of us.

As someone who has walked this path, I understand the courage it takes to face our fears of rejection and to choose joy and laughter in their stead. This choice, though it may seem small, is a powerful act of self-love and acceptance.

I encourage you to take the lessons and practices shared in these pages and integrate them into your daily life. Let humor be your shield, joy your compass, and playfulness your constant

companion. The road may have its twists and turns, but it's a road worth traveling.

Remember, you are not alone in this journey. As a life coach and fellow traveler on this path, I remain committed to supporting and guiding those who grapple with the complexities of RSD. Together, we can turn our sensitivities into our greatest strengths, finding light in moments of darkness and laughter in places of silence.

Thank you for joining me on this playful path. May your journey be filled with joyous discoveries and gentle acceptance of your beautiful, sensitive self.

With
warmth
and grati-
tude, Am-
manuel
Santa
Anna

Ammanuel Santa Anna is a seasoned life coach and author with a profound understanding of the human psyche. With over 20 years of experience in self-help and a solid background in applied psychology spanning a decade, Ammanuel has dedicated his career to empowering individuals to overcome their challenges and achieve their full potential. His expertise is particularly notable in the realm of Rejection Sensitive Dysphoria (RSD), a condition he has navigated personally and professionally. This unique perspective enriches his approach, making him a compassionate and effective coach who genuinely understands the struggles of those he helps.